RORY MOULTON

53 Paris Travel Tips

Secrets, Advice & Insight for a Perfect Paris Vacation

First edition

ISBN: 978-1-7287063-6-8

This book was professionally typeset on Reedsy.
Find out more at reedsy.com

Contents

III   PART 3: INDULGE

FREE Paris eBook

Receive a FREE Paris ebook today.

After downloading your free book, you'll receive a monthly VIP email with book giveaways, new book announcements and huge book discounts ONLY available exclusively to subscribers.

Join the crew and subscribe for FREE to Rory Moulton's monthly email newsletter about European travel, "EuroExperto." In addition to the giveaways and discounts, receive the month's best European travel articles, news, tips, trends and more. I'll never spam you. I don't do ads. And you can unsubscribe at any time.

Smarter European travel is just a click away: www.rorymoulton.com

Also by Rory Moulton

Other works available from the author:
- 53 Amsterdam Travel Tips
- Paris with Kids
- Washington, DC with Kids
- 99 Things To Do in Paris with Kids

Introduction

"Paris, however – because of her purely fortuitous beauty, because of the old things which have become a part of her, because of her entanglement of buildings and tenements – Paris yields herself in discovery as an attic beloved in our childhood gave up its secrets."
  Jean Cocteau, The Paris We Love

Few cities on Earth induce such passion, such wonderment as Paris. France's capital, long drawing artists, writers, bon vivants, world leaders, fashionistas and travelers, holds an unassailable position in the hearts and minds of all who have ever strolled her tangled streets.

There's simply something about Paris. It's not only the plethora of illustrious art, seemingly endless museum halls, historic ghosts or acclaimed café scene. Paris seems to create its own heartbeat that, much like the mysterious attic of our childhood years that Jean Cocteau references, holds a fascinating allure; the city invites you to tap this vein and forever see the world and yourself differently.

But if Paris is like a beloved attic from our childhood, it is becoming an increasingly crowded one. More than 15 million international tourists descend on the city every year. It's now imperative for savvy travelers to make the necessary reservations, beat the tour groups and seek out lesser-known, "secret" spots.

In *53 Paris Travel Tips*, I dispense my very best advice for traveling Paris. Gleaned from over 15 years of travels to the great City of Light, my secrets and insight will help you plan and execute the perfect Paris getaway. You'll learn how to skip crowds, find the city's best values and experience the city more like a savvy local than a bewildered tourist. Whether it's your first time in Paris or you're back for more, this book will teach you something new.

I

PART 1: SURVIVE & THRIVE

1

Bonjour! (French for the Rest of Us)

A t shops, restaurants and market stalls it's customary, even obligatory, to greet staff with a heartfelt *"Bonjour!"* immediately upon entering and *"Au revoir!"* before leaving (fake it if you must, which might be the most important Parisian social skill of all). This is expected behavior in Paris and throughout France. Even little kids do it. You will, too.

But this advice comes with a caveat: As much as "the French" love to hear tourists attempting to speak "the French," this is a busy, hustle-and-bustle city – shop clerks, waiters, bartenders and the like are not your free language tutors. Lead with and use the French you have, but don't expect help or praise for trying. And don't bother asking for language tips.

Don't worry, though: You're going to nail down some indispensable phrases and stride confidently through Paris' open markets, boutique shops and endless cafés. And just to reassure you, most Parisians will stoop to speaking English with you, no matter how reluctantly.

So, let's just master basic pleasantries and a few survival

phrases – no need to study for the French AP exam. Nail these phrases and you'll quickly separate yourself from Paris' tourist morass:

- Hello :: **Bonjour ::** *Bohn-zhoor.*
- Goodbye :: **Au revoir ::** *Oh vwahr.*
- Thank you :: **Merci ::** *Mehr-see.*
- Yes, please :: **Oui, s'il vous plait ::** *Wee see voo play.*
- Excuse me :: **Pardon ::** *Par-dohn.*
- Do you speak English? :: **Parlez-vous anglais?** :: *Par-lay-voo ahn-glay?*
- The check please. :: **L'addition s'il vous plait.** :: *Ler diss-ee-ohn see voo play.*
- Where are the toilets? :: **Où sont les toilettes?** :: *Oo sohn lay twah-leht?*
- How much is it? :: **Combien?** :: *Kohn-bee-an?*
- Where is _____? :: **Où est _____?** :: *Oo ay?*
- I'd like _____. :: **Je voudrais _____.** :: *Zhuh voo-dray.*
- 1, 2, 3, 4, 5, half-kilo :: Un, deux, trois, quatre, cinq, demi-kilo. :: *Uhn, duh, twah, kah-truh, sank, deu-mee key-low.*

2

Six Killer Apps

Traveling to Paris isn't about staying buried in your phone, but a handful of key apps will make the trip smoother and more enjoyable. General travel apps abound, but I suggest keeping it light with:

- Google Translate
- Google Maps
- Kindle (or whatever ebook reading app you prefer)
- TripIt (for organizing your itinerary)

That's about it. Save storage space for photos, videos and these six killer apps designed specifically for Paris:

1. Next Stop Paris: iTunes + Android

2. RATP: iTunes + Android

Next Stop Paris and the RATP apps provide updated information on train timetables, station closures, transit strikes and will geolocate the closest Metro stations. Both are recommended for efficiently riding the easy public-transit system.

3. My Visit to the Louvre: iTunes + Android

It's the official, official Louvre app. This app features 3D floor plans, maps, suggested itineraries, an artwork and artist search engine and over 600 descriptions, and audio commentary. Phew! That's almost as exhausting as the museum itself. Speaking of, the Louvre is massive and crowded. This app helps you navigate around the endless corridors, confusing stairwells and, perhaps most importantly, helps prioritize what you want to see. Cuz you ain't gonna see it all. Unless you move to Paris.

4. Le Fooding: iTunes

Find trendy restaurants and honest, Parisian-reviewed eateries near you using geolocation with this groundbreaking app built from the popular website. It's easy to use, constantly updated and gives an insider's view on a huge inventory of Parisian restaurants. It's your go-to food-recommendation app for Paris.

5. Secrets de Paris: iTunes + Android

This fun app, run by a team of longtime Parisians, reveals a little-known place or activity every day. You can save "secrets" for later, and the app uses geolocation to plot routes to your saved "secrets." Definitely download this app at least a few weeks prior to your trip so you can build a robust list.

6. L'Instant Parisien: iTunes + Android

I really love L'Instant Parisien's portraits of the city's inhabitants, off-the-beaten-track suggestions and the creative, intimate city walks they publish weekly.

3

Never Get Lost

P aris, as every travel writer past, present or future will undoubtedly claim, is a collection of neighborhoods. I'm sure I've written it. In fact, I just did. And that's because it's an accurate observation. (But, really, what major city isn't a collection of distinct enclaves...?)

To grasp the layout of Paris, you must understand three key elements and how they relate geographically: 1) the River Seine that bisects the city, 2) the "*arrondissements*" (municipal clusters of neighborhoods) that swirl outward from the Seine like a snail shell and 3) the Boulevard Périphérique that encompasses it all. Know how these three geographic elements work in relation to one another and you'll never get lost. At least not for long.

Let's start in the bull's-eye center, where it all started. The historic heart of Paris centers on two islands in the Seine – Île de la Cité and Île Saint-Louis – where the Celtic Parisii tribe first settled some 2,500 years ago. Île de la Cité is home to titanic attractions. Notre-Dame flanks the southeast end, Pont Neuf mans the northwest end and Sainte-Chapelle sits in between.

Southeast, or upriver, from Île de la Cité, rests the quieter Île Saint-Louis.

Paris is divided into the Left and Right Banks by the river – the Left Bank is south of the Seine and the Right Bank is north of the Seine. For reference, here are some popular attractions and neighborhoods organized by Left and Right Banks.

Left Bank: Eiffel Tower, The Catacombs, Jardin du Luxembourg, Musée d'Orsay, Musée de l'Armée/Invalides.

Right Bank: Marais, Centre Pompidou, Musée d'Orsay, Avenue des Champs-Élysées, Père Lachaise cemetery.

The Seine is Paris' "*raison d'être*," its original geo-economic engine. Paris occupies a strategic crossroads on the Seine – the intersection of land- and sea-based trade routes that have converged on the Île de la Cité since Celtic tribes first settled France, then known as Gaul (at least to the Romans). The Seine runs from southeast to northwest through Paris making a big left turn near the Eiffel Tower on its way to the English Channel (or "*la Manche*" – literally, "the sleeve" – as the Channel is known in France) at Le Havre and Honfleur on the Normandy coast. Or, in travel terms, the Seine flows from Notre-Dame Cathedral toward the Eiffel Tower.

Okay, you're square on the Seine and how it bifurcates the city. Let's now look at the arrondissements and where they sit in relation to the Seine and the city as a whole.

From the Seine, Paris radiates outward into 20 districts or arrondissements contained within the ring road, Boulevard Périphérique. Arrondissements are commonly abbreviated with their respective number and the letter "e" which is short for *ème*, equivalent to the –nd and –rd suffixes in English ordinal numbers like 2nd and 3rd. The only exception is the first arrondissement, which is abbreviated "1er" for "premier."

Everything inside Boulevard Périphérique is considered Paris proper; everything outside is considered the suburbs, the "*agglomération Parisienne.*" For travelers to Paris, most noteworthy sites are within the Boulevard Périphérique in one of the 20 arrondissements.

The 20 arrondissements begin in the historic city center with the other 19 spiraling out clockwise from there. Arrondissements 5-7 and 13-15 are located on the Left Bank, while 1-4, 8-12 and 16-20 sit on the Right Bank.

On the Right Bank, 1er contains the Louvre, Palais Royale and Tuileries but also Île de la Cité and Île Saint-Louis. 2e is due north of 1er, still on the Right Bank, but beginning to curve eastward into 3e and 4e, but due east of 2e. 5e jumps the Seine south of 4e to the Left Bank, while 6e and 7e continue the westward spiral on the Left Bank.

This spiral or "snail" numbering system continues to the 20th arrondissement, which, starting with arrondissement 12, borders the Boulevard Périphérique, the outermost fringe of Paris proper. If all this sounds confusing, Google "Paris arrondissement map" and then reread the paragraph with your new visual aid.

Parisian addresses almost always include the arrondissement number after the street address. Let's check out an example to see how this works in real life. Take the following address: 62 rue de Lille, 7e. It means the location is at building number 62 on Lille Street in Paris' 7th arrondissement. Rue = street, and is not capitalized like in English addresses.

(Oh, and by the way, 62 rue de Lille is the physical address of the Musée d'Orsay, which is an address worth remembering. Hint, hint...)

4

Metro Like a Local

You'll enjoy lovely walks every day in Paris, linking your walks with the Metro – Paris' efficient and easy-to-use subway system. Buses are also abundant, and convenient RER surface trains offer suburban service to places like Versailles.

Within the city circle, all tickets work on all modes of public transportation – bus, Metro and RER trains. Most of your sightseeing also happens to be in the city center. Therefore, if you decline to buy the rather expensive Paris Visite pass that covers unlimited public transportation for 1, 2, 3 or 5 consecutive days, then you'll definitely want to purchase a "carnet" of 10 "T+" tickets. You can purchase carnets at the ticket vending machines near the Metro turnstiles.

Download the **Next Stop Paris – RATP apps** (see Six Killer Apps chapter) for updated timetables, strike info, station closures and more. These are two of Paris' best apps and super handy for plotting your path across the city.

The Metro subway system serves all of Paris with quick, easy, reliable and safe service. It seems like you're never more than a few minutes from a Metro stop. The Metro system is broken into five zones, with zone 1 in the center of Paris and the other four zones radiating outward from there. Travelers like us primarily utilize zone 1 and rarely travel beyond zone 3 (Versailles).

Buy tickets at easy-to-use, English-language machines (coins or credit) or at *possibly* English-speaking ticket sellers available at larger stations (cash or credit) near the turnstiles. Insert your ticket at the turnstile and wait for the automated gate signal to turn green, and then proceed through. Don't forget to retrieve your ticket at the other end!

The system map is clearly displayed in all stations and all train cars show the route on which you're traveling. Whatever map you choose – I'll be using the Streetwise Paris map in my hands and Google Maps on my phone – it should at least show all the major Metro stops within the 20 arrondissements. Despite the color and number, lines are almost always referred to by their end-of-the-line stops, so get used to following the little colored lines to their endpoints.

Plotting your course is easy: Find the closest station to you, then find the station nearest your destination and pick the line or lines that connects them. Be sure to note any closed stations on your route to minimize surprises.

Remember: Each line has trains traveling in either direction. Line up on the side of the station that says the name of the end station in the direction you wish to go. Then confirm this on the digital sign on the first train car as it enters the station. Again, you want to travel in the direction *toward* the end station at or after your destination, not away from it. I've definitely never made that mistake and am 100% not speaking from experience...

5

Safety Meeting

aris is as safe as big cities get, but like any major city it does have some petty theft and scam artists, though relatively little in the way of violent crime. Pickpockets and scam artists are the tourist's main concerns. You shall remain ever vigilant!

Pickpockets operate in crowded areas in and around major attractions and on public transportation – be careful while waiting in line, keep your valuables in a money belt or a hidden, zippered pocket, and be vigilant in crowds. On the Metro, hop on the first or last car on a train since they are almost always less crowded and thus less susceptible to pickpockets.

You must strive to blend in! The goal isn't necessarily to look like a Parisian – that takes decades of careful study and preparation – but to look like a savvy tourist. Sorry, you're leaving the black socks, Birkenstocks and fanny packs at home. Don't flash your guidebook around. Don't thumb through wads of cash out in public. Assess your appearance before wading into the tourist morass – do you look like a tourist? Are you dressed like other Parisians – simply yet elegantly put together with classic styling?

In sum, the best pickpocket deterrent is to keep your valuables close, look like you belong and keep open an eagle eye out for suspicious-looking individuals. Do those three things and you'll be just fine, virtually pickpocket-proof.

Now for the scammers.

One of the most popular scams involves a heister offering to "help" purchase a Metro ticket. Scammers wait for obvious tourists by automated ticket machines and quickly sidle up to the unsuspecting prey, offering friendly aid in purchasing tickets. They say they're buying you a Metro pass good for multiple trips or a week, but instead order you a one-ride ticket and pocket the significant difference. If confronted with such an offer, firmly say no and proceed to purchase tickets using the English-language machines. You got this.

On a recent trip, two Americans in my hotel lobby, jet lag washed across their poor faces, were showing the front desk attendant the one-ride tickets they had thought were one-week, all-you-can-ride tickets (which don't exist). They were victims of a scam artist who pocketed a couple hundred euros from the poor couple while pretending to help them use the ticket machine. You don't need help: Take your time and read the machine (they display in English), choosing the ticket that suits your needs.

Another common scam is the petition scam. I've personally experienced this in Notre-Dame's plaza. Young people with clipboards – sometimes kids – will ask you to sign a petition for such-and-such program and then ask for a donation. Do not sign anything. In fact, ignore them and walk away. They are part of a syndicate that exploits tourists for profit – they are not raising money for such-and-such organization. Repeat: Walk away. Or do as I do and spout nonsense angrily in what little German you may know. That also seems to do the trick.

Other scams in tourist areas typically come disguised as unsolicited help. A smart traveler stays on-guard and aware. Sadly, a good rule of thumb is if the person is going out of their way to help you for seemingly little-to-no reward and are offering the help unsolicited, then they probably want something clandestinely in return. Be smart, be aware and be self-sufficient.

6

Cash is King

France, like most countries in the European Union, uses the euro, €. The euro sign is usually placed after the amount and a comma is used where North Americans employ the decimal point. For example, a coffee that costs 4.50 euros will be written as 4,50€. But here's where it gets a little convoluted: When written in English, the euro sign is placed before the amount, so this little book adheres to that usage guideline.

Cash is still king in Paris – especially at the small, family run establishments favored by me and listed in this book. Even at big chains, small purchases are expected to be made in cash and plastic is reserved for large purchases. Many small hotels and some travel agencies offer a 5-10% discount for cash payment. Plan to use cash for most non-restaurant meals and carry several different small bills because...

Surprise! Parisian shop clerks prefer exact change or a round number close to the total so they don't have to fuss with breaking euros. Being asked by clerks for exact change or a rounder sum can be surprising – to Americans especially, where the customer can do no wrong and businesses are expected to bend over backwards for clients – but Parisians prefer practicality (at least when it comes to making change... Women's shoes? Not so much.). Breaking a big bill for a small purchase or scrounging up a heap of change doesn't make sense to logical minds if a tidier transaction can be done. Phew, that's a long-winded way of saying it's good form to carry small bills, an array of change and one-euro coins (also handy for pay toilets).

Your ATM card should work just fine in Paris. ATMs are the best way to withdraw cash – the rates and fees are far better than doing currency exchange or using traveler's checks. Since you have a daily withdrawal limit and you don't want to spend your first moments in Paris hunting for an ATM, order euros from your bank, usually for no extra charge, several weeks before departure. I use Wells Fargo and like to depart with at least €1,000.

7

The Toilette Quest

Though the authorities are belatedly addressing the problem, the public toilet situation in Paris is, well, in a word: inconvenient. There are nowhere near enough public toilets and the majority are automated toilets, so already-lengthy wait times become even longer due to the automated toilets running their excruciatingly protracted cleaning cycle.

Don't fret. I'm here to help and, really, it's but a matter of a little foresight and diligence. Follow my tried-and-true rule of thumb: Use the bathroom twice at every attraction or restaurant – once upon arrival and once before departing. No questions asked. Well, maybe there will be one question asked.

To ask for the toilets, say, *"Où sont les toilettes?"* (Oo sohn lay twah-leht). Sometimes the WCs cost a euro or two (I know, I know, you paid to get in and now you must pay to pee. Such is life!), but it's well worth it, and a compelling reason to carry around one-euro coins on your person. Otherwise, public bathrooms remain scarce and lines to use them can be painfully long.

To locate those elusive public *toilettes*, look for oblong, green free-standing stalls – automated JCDecaux toilets – usually tucked between busy roads and bustling sidewalks. As mentioned, these public bathrooms are fully automated and self-cleaning, so they go through an automatic cleaning cycle between each user. The status of the *toilette* – vacant, occupied or cleaning – is displayed on a panel beside the door. Do not try to sneak in between users – you'll get soaked. There are 400 automated WCs scattered about, which hardly suffices for a city so large and so slammed with tourists. Again, though, the authorities claim to be addressing this shortcoming. We won't hold our collective breaths, or any other bodily functions.

And when all else fails – you're in between museums and can't find a public toilet – confidently stroll into a café like you're coming from one of their outside tables, say bonjour to the wait staff and head toward the restrooms in the back. Busy Parisian waiters and bartenders are unlikely to interfere. But if they do, plunk down a few euros for an espresso at the bar. Alas, the cycle begins anew.

8

Free Wi-Fi

You gotta stay connected in Paris, pulling up Google Maps, checking email and, of course, posting sick photos to Instagram! Luckily, Paris has 400 free Wi-Fi points around parks, libraries and major attractions. Find a free network at Paris.fr or look for the maroon Paris "Wi-Fi" logo.

When you're in one of the city's free Wi-Fi zones, select the "Orange" network from the list of available networks. Launch a web browser and type in any web address. A prompt will appear (in French) asking you to select a "pass Paris Wi-Fi 2h." Click on the pass and you're connected! You will now be able to surf for up to two hours, after which you'll need to reactivate the pass. Note, however, that Paris city Wi-Fi hotspots are only available during daytime.

Most, if not all, parks listed in this book offer free Wi-Fi. Many large attractions, like the Centre Georges Pompidou, and most popular cafes also dish out free Wi-Fi.

Without a doubt, Paris' free Wi-Fi network is among the world's best free hotspots. Now, if you could only convince them to add 400 more free public toilets...

II

PART 2: GO >> SEE >> DO

9

One Pass to Rule Them All

S ince you're fixing to see three or more museums or monuments, buy the Paris Museum Pass (PMP) for everyone in your party 18 years and older. PMP holders gain entry to some of Paris' best museums for free (list below), bypassing ticket lines. In fact, it's worth buying just to skip the ticket lines alone. Many sights in this book accept the Paris Museum Pass, though the Eiffel Tower, Natural History Museum and Catacombs are notable exceptions.

The pass comes in three consecutive-day increments: €48 for two days, €62 for four days and €74 for six days (prices accurate as of publication, but check online here for current pricing). Doing the math to determine which pass will work best is easy. First, decide which sights you're highly likely to see using the list below. Then, carefully check their respective websites to calculate the total tickets costs. Finally, using that sum total, decide which pass makes financial sense and best fits your itinerary. And just to reiterate: Even if the math doesn't quite justify buying a PMP based on admission prices, but comes close, it's still worth it for the line-jumping privileges.

There's no need to buy the pass online in advance because you must pick it up anyway. Buy yours at a tabac (tobacco shop), news kiosk or tourist information office instead of a museum to avoid lines altogether. Use the Paris Museum Pass website to locate a retailer near your lodging and buy it during your "First Impressions" stroll after check-in (see next chapter). If there isn't a convenient location nearby, then you can grab it at Paris Charles de Gaulle Airport, your arrival train station, or at any tabac en route to your first attraction.

Validate the pass at the first site by writing the day's date and signing the back before approaching the entrance. The pass is good for consecutive days; you'll only validate it when you're ready to begin your heavy sightseeing, likely day two.

On arrival at your first site, you can head straight to the main entrance, showing your passes to the guard, who will let you right in – as if you were museum royalty! Even at places like the Arc de Triomphe or Rodin Museum, where it's not apparent how to get around the line, just elbow your way through and flash the PMP to the attendant. You're sure to be ushered right through. Remember: You pay for the right to skip the line, so don't shy away from exercising the privilege.

Paris Museum Passes are no-brainers for those big-time sightseeing days – the only question is which pass, two, four or six days. Check the Paris Museum Pass website for current pricing and the most up-to-date list of included sights and purchase locations.

Check this list. Going to three or more? Buy a Paris Museum Pass. My recommended sights are in bold.

IN PARIS
Arc de Triomphe

Musée de l'Armée - Tombeau de Napoléon 1er

Centre Pompidou - Musée National d'Art Moderne

Musée National des Arts asiatiques – Guimet

Musée des Arts décoratifs

Espaces Mode et Textile

Espaces Publicité

Musée Nissim de Camondo

Musée des Arts et Métiers

Musée du quai Branly – Jacques Chirac

Chapelle expiatoire

La Cinémathèque Française – Musée du Cinéma

Cité des Sciences et de l'Industrie – universcience

Conciergerie

Musée national Eugène Delacroix

Visite publique des Égouts de Paris

Palais de la Porte Dorée – Musée national de l'histoire de l'Immigration

Musée de l'Institut du Monde arabe

Musée d'art et d'histoire du Judaïsme

Musée du Louvre

Cité de l'Architecture et du Patrimoine – Musée des Monuments français

Musée Gustave Moreau

Musée de Cluny – Musée national du Moyen Âge

Philharmonie de Paris – Musée de la musique

Crypte archéologique du Parvis Notre-Dame

Tours de Notre-Dame

Musée national de l'Orangerie

Musée de l'Ordre de la Libération

Musée d'Orsay

Palais de la découverte – universcience

Panthéon

Musée national Picasso-Paris

Musée des Plans-reliefs

Musée Rodin

Sainte-Chapelle

OUTSIDE PARIS

Musée de l'Air et de l'Espace

Musée d'Archéologie nationale et Domaine national de Saint-Germain-en-Laye

Sèvres, Cité de la céramique – Musée national de la céramique

Abbaye royale de Chaalis

Château de Champs-sur-Marne

Musées et domaine nationaux du Palais de Compiègne

Musée Condé – Château de Chantilly

Musée départemental Maurice Denis

Château de Fontainebleau

Château de Maisons

Musée national du château de Malmaison

Château de Pierrefonds

Musée national de Port-Royal des Champs

Château de Rambouillet, Laiterie de la Reine et Chaumière aux Coquillages

Musée national de la Renaissance – Château d'Ecouen

Maison d'Auguste Rodin à Meudon

Basilique cathédrale de Saint-Denis

Villa Savoye

Châteaux de Versailles et de Trianon

Château de Vincennes

10

Do You Have a Reservation? Part 1

The Paris Museum Pass doesn't cover every attraction and there will be sightseeing days before and after you activate the pass. Additionally, you may not want to see enough museums to warrant a PMP; there are many, many cafés, after all. In these instances, you're absolutely going to try to book your tickets online in advance. By booking tickets online for as many attractions as possible and purchasing a Paris Museum Pass you're going to waltz into Paris' top attractions like you own them. Say au revoir to horrendous ticket-buying lines and bonjour to stress-free Paris!

So what reservations do you need and when do you get them? First, list all the sights you're definitely going to see. Next, determine which of those attractions are included on the PMP and which ones you'll realistically have time to see. Now those leftovers, which probably include the Eiffel Tower and Catacombs, are your reservation targets.

Not all attractions offer online tickets and some – like the Catacombs – charge an exorbitant fee for online ticketing. Catacombs reservations cost more than double what normal tickets cost, but online tickets do include the excellent audioguide. Unfortunately, this is the only way around the Catacombs' long line, so queue up by 9:15AM if you don't have a reservation. During high season, it's definitely worth considering an online Catacombs ticket.

Eiffel Tower tickets become available online 90 days in advance and usually sell out within a few minutes of the day they go on sale. Literally, a few minutes. Log in to your computer and have the order ready – date and time required. When it is 8:30AM Paris time, press Submit. The alternative is to forgo a reservation and take the stairs – discussed later or...

11

When All Else Fails

Money not a problem? Like to be spontaneous? Forgot to make a reservation? The damn Eiffel Tower tickets came and went before you could even open your laptop? Don't worry. There are still line-hopping tickets available for those of us living life on the edge.

Score those elusive line-jumping tickets ("*coup-file*") from tourist information offices, FNAC department stores and private tour companies, though expect a significant – *significant* – surcharge. I'm talking at least twice the sticker price. *Coup-file* tickets are limited and aren't always available for the days and times you want, so it may take a few attempts before landing tickets to your liking. And you may need to refinance the house in order to do so.

12

First Impressions

You've landed in Paris and your first task (after a jetlag-combating snack and coffee, of course) is to get acquainted with the city, get a feel for its layout and capture a bird's-eye view of the winding urban garden you're about to explore. Also, you need some fresh air and exercise to stave off the aforementioned jetlag.

First, you need to gain some elevation. Luckily, Paris is great at first impressions. The City of Light is teeming with amazing viewpoints, the best of which are, in no particular order:

- The Pompidou Centre's top floor (6th) accessed via the inside-out escalators.
- Notre-Dame Cathedral's rooftop, accessed via the tower climb.
- The Eiffel Tower (duh) offers commanding views from the 2nd and top levels.
- Sacré Coeur's rooftop, accessed via the tower climb.
- Arc de Triomphe.
- Montparnasse Tower.
- La Grande Arche – the only viewpoint listed here that lies

outside downtown Paris.

- Musée d'Orsay's roof deck, adjacent to the Café Campana on the 5th floor.
- The rooftop terraces of department stores Printemps and Galeries Lafayette.

For your first elevated look at Paris, you needn't be picky. Find the closest viewpoint listed above or the one that best fits your first-day itinerary and go. Climb to the top and take it all in. Your Paris adventure begins.

13

Rise and Shine

Get up early because Paris – especially during high tourist season – is not kind to those who sleep in. Line-choked Paris can quickly discourage travelers with interminable wait times and shoulder-to-shoulder crowds. Fancy feeling like a sardine? Go to the Orsay Museum right after lunch.

But you're not a sardine. You're a human being and you can outsmart the herds. Yes, the herds. You see, most tourists visit Paris on group tours and those group tours really pack 'em in, sometimes 80+ people per tour. Once those tour buses start arriving at attractions, the lines quickly become unbearable. Your goal is to beat the tour buses every morning. Arrive at the day's first attraction a solid 15 minutes before it opens.

Churches are great first stops because they typically open their doors to the public by 8AM. You can see a church and still make a 10AM museum opening – freeing up your post-lunch itinerary for... well, anything other than waiting in line. Picnics. Lesser-known museums and attractions. Walking. Shopping. People watching. Café hopping. You get the picture: Get up early, hit the big attractions first, then find a café or park bench and let the rest of the day find you.

14

Free Orientation

There's nothing quite like a guided walk to orient yourself to a new city. All the better if that tour is free. These free city tours really are just overview tours – they're not intended for folks seeking an in-depth city or themed tour, and repeat visitors will see little value in them. It's an orientation, so set your expectations low and they will be met. It's worth your time on a first visit to Paris. For freshmen only!

A quick note about free: As Pops always said, "There's no such thing as a free lunch." So, while these tours have no upfront costs, guides do expect a cash tip at the tour's conclusion. Five euros per person is sufficient.

Here are two recommended companies giving free Paris tours:

· Discover Walks
· City Free Tour

15

Sunday Funday Free Day

It's the first (Sunday) of the month and you're in Paris, which means you're in luck. The City of Light kicks off each month with a host of freebies – a bunch of museums go free and the Avenue des Champs-Élysées goes car-free. Some museums only offer free first Sundays during non-peak season, generally fall through early spring; the months in which they participate in free first Sundays are noted below in parentheses.

Without further ado, here it is, a comprehensive list of free first Sundays in Paris:

Musée National d'Art Moderne (Centre Pompidou)

Musée de l'Assistance Publique

Musée des Arts et Métiers

Musée de la Chasse et de la Nature

Musée national Eugène Delacroix

Musée national Gustave Moreau

Musée national Ernest Hébert Hôtel de Montmorency-Bours

Musée national Jean-Jacques Henner

Musée national du Moyen Âge

Musée national de l'Orangerie

Musée d'Orsay

Musée national Picasso

Cité de l'Architecture et du Patrimoine

Cité nationale de l'histoire de l'immigration

Musée du Quai Branly

Musée national des Arts asiatiques Guimet

Musée du Louvre (October–March)

Musée Rodin (October–March)

Conciergerie (November–March)

Panthéon (November–March)

Sainte-Chapelle (November–March)

Tours de Notre-Dame (November–March)

Château de Vincennes (November–March)

Château de Versailles (November–March)

Arc de Triomphe (November–March)

Champs-Élysées: Ever wanted to recreate the final leg of the Tour de France? Or simply stroll along this iconic street without dodging cars? As part of an anti-smog program, Paris began banning cars on the Champs-Élysées on the first Sunday of every month in 2016, to coincide with free museum day. It's quite a sight to behold: one of Paris' busiest thoroughfares with nary a motorized vehicle in sight, only walkers, bikers, skateboarders and rollerbladers.

While I'm not a big fan of the retail nightmare that is the Champs-Élysées, if you're in Paris on that first Sunday, then you'll be strolling the Champs-Élysées with hardly a car around... after hitting up a free museum of course!

16

Kids Go Gratis

Anyone under 18 and EU citizens under 26 receive free admission to so many of Paris' top museums it's obnoxious. As a general rule of thumb, under 18s don't need a Paris Museum Pass and receive free admission to the national museums and monuments, which doesn't include, per usual, the Eiffel Tower and Catacombs.

Here's the list:

Musée du Louvre

Musée national Jean-Jacques Henner

Musée national Eugène Delacroix

Musée national Gustave Moreau

Musée Rodin

Musée d'Orsay

Musée national des Arts asiatiques Guimet

Musée du quai Branly – Jacques Chirac

Cité de l'Architecture et du Patrimoine

Cité nationale de l'histoire de l'immigration

Musée national du Moyen Âge

Musée national de l'Orangerie

Musée national Picasso

Musée National d'Art Moderne (Centre Pompidou)

Musée de l'Armée

Les Arts Décoratifs Les Arts Décoratifs –– Nissim de Camondo

Musée des Arts et Métiers

Musée national de la Marine

Musée de la Poste

Musée de la Musique – Philharmonie de Paris

Arc de Triomphe

Chapelle expiatoire

Conciergerie

Tours de Notre-Dame

Panthéon

Sainte-Chapelle

Musée des Plans et Reliefs

Musée d'art et d'histoire du Judaïsme

Grande Galerie de l'Evolution

Institut du Monde Arabe

17

Globe Envy

Today, you're hunting one of Paris' lesser-known treasures. You know, the ones without hordes of tourists taking selfies out front.

France's spectacular National Library (itself a hidden gem), home to over 10 million books, contains two of the world's most impressive globes. These 20-foot monsters originally belonged to Louis XIV, who commissioned them after jealousy seeing his friend, the Duke of Parma, show off his own huge globes. Globe envy, amirite?

Just beholding these wondrous and curious globes makes a trip to the library worth it. From Atlas Obscura:

> *"One globe depicts the cosmos with astrological constella-*
> *tions. The stars are arranged as they would have appeared*
> *at the date of Louis XIV's birth in September of 1638. It*
> *places the Earth at the center of the solar system, a widely*
> *accepted theory at the time. The second globe depicts*
> *the continents of the Earth with exotic illustrations of the*
> *people who live across the world. These were intended to*

provide encyclopedic information about whalers in the Pacific, tribesmen in Africa, cannibals in Brazil (from the accounts of Amerigo Vespucci), among others. It serves as a literal manifestation of Louis XIV's worldview, and provides an image of how we believed the world looked in the 1680s."

On public display only since 2009, find them at the main branch, the François-Mitterrand Library on Quai François-Mauriac at 25 rue Emile Durkheim (climbing the stairs) or via the avenue de France. Get there before the selfie-taking hordes do.

18

Commune Art

Y ou know what you're not going to do? Overpay for art just because you're at one of Paris' touristic art-buying locations, like the grossly commercial Tertre Square in Montmartre. Thanks, but no thanks. To score affordable, original and brilliant canvases, you're going to a commune.

Unless you're a serious art collector seeking expensive pieces or, conversely, are happy getting swindled by artists in popular tourist areas (ahem, once again I'm looking at you Place du Tertre), then the best place for normal people to buy quality Parisian art is the artists' collective known as 59 Rivoli, which is also conveniently the building's address: 59 rue Rivoli (not far from the Louvre).

The collective's up-and-coming, live-in artists display their work for sale in the ground-floor gallery. You won't overpay here and you won't find portrait artists displaying their best Brad Pitt caricature. 59 Rivoli is for serious, up-and-coming artists ready to strike a deal on an original canvas.

19

Kitschy Cabaret

S cantily clad women and men throwing up their heels, doing the cancan, twirling through the air, dancing in kick lines all while wearing something that could easily make a peacock blush – what fun!

Well, for some, just the thought of a cabaret makes them feel uneasy. Thongs? Men in compression shorts? Bare-breasted women? Oh, those hedonistic French! Cabaret can't possibly be for us, right? Wrong.

You've got to see one cabaret show while in Paris, so you might as well see the kitschiest, if not the most amusing. In operation since 1803, the Paradis Latin Cabaret is a heck of a lot of cheesy fun. It's far less touristy and expensive than the better-known Moulin Rouge, but the shows here are just flat-out entertaining, the food is better and everything just feels more... well, French.

Can you let down your guard and enjoy a night at a Parisian cabaret? Yes, yes you cancan.

20

Hop-on, Hop-off River Cruising

Some European cities – okay, *most* European cities – have some form of hop-on, hop-off buses and river boats for tourists that stop at all the usual sites. Since public transit is cheaper and more widespread, I'm not a big fan of these services. Except in Paris.

In Paris, grab a day pass on the Batobus, the comfortable barges methodically plying the Seine, stopping at nine popular attractions on the Left and Right Banks: Eiffel Tower, Orsay Museum, Saint Germain, Notre-Dame, Jardin des Plantes, Hotel De Ville, Louvre, Champs-Élysées and Beaugrenelle. You'll get on and off at your leisure, while resting your feet in between sites. The glass-dome roofs allow an unobstructed, water-level view of historic Paris you can't get anywhere else.

Sure you're a Metro expert now, but you're also not immune to a little pampering. Plus, wow, the view. Did I mention the view? You gotta see the view.

21

Bike Like a Local

Parisians, like their urban Western European counter-parts, are working to make their city more bike friendly. While it's no Amsterdam, certain areas of Paris are lovely for biking, including along the Seine, in the 7e and through many parks. While it may be tempting to rent a bike from a tour company or overpay at a rental shop catering to tourists, there's a cheaper and more efficient option: bike sharing.

Paris is home to the world's largest bike-sharing program, "Vélib'". Instead of renting an overpriced bike from a tour company, sign up online for a Vélib' account to pay less than two euros a day. Plus, you can pick up and drop off at any of their 1,800 Paris locations, taking as many one-way trips as you'd like.

Here's how it works:

1. Go to a computer terminal at any Vélib' station or purchase a one-day or seven-day pass online.
2. Follow the on-screen instructions, available in English. If this is your first rental and you haven't booked online, then

you'll first create an account with a security pin number.

3. Select a bike from the rack and note its number – check first that the brakes, pedals, tires and seat are in proper working order – and select the bike number from the screen. If the bike you want isn't showing as available, then it's probably broken or wasn't properly returned.

4. Wait for the green light and two-beep signal and take your bike when it's automatically unlocked from the rack.

5. When returning your bike at any station (it doesn't have to be returned to where you rented it), be sure the bike is properly checked back in and locked correctly. Otherwise, the system will think you still have a bike checked out. Wait for the green "success" light and print a return-confirmation receipt.

Affordable + convenient = Vélib'.

22

The One-Hour Rule

O n those long summer and spring evenings, it's hard to resist the urge to squeeze in one more museum. So don't. If you've still got spring in your step, a-sightseeing you will go. But you've got to keep an eye on the clock.

One of Paris' unwritten rules can make or break your evening. Museums and attractions post their official closing time and that's the time they kick you out of the museum. What's not posted, but will often be mentioned on the website, is the time they close their doors to new guests, usually 30-45 minutes before the official closing time.

To be safe, follow a one-hour rule: Arrive at least 60 minutes before closing time to ensure entry. That way, even if you run into one of Paris' notoriously prickly museum workers, you'll still give yourself a little cushion. If you can't make the Orsay or Orangerie one hour before closing time, then all's not lost: It's likely primetime in the cafés.

23

Eiffel Tower the Awesome Way

irst time visiting the Eiffel Tower? Be sure to take the stairs. The Eiffel Tower's stairs route isn't nearly as terrifying as it sounds – the stairs are safely enclosed inside metal caging within the south pillar, "*pilier sud.*"

It's impossible to reserve stairs tickets in advance, but the line is always a small fraction of the size of the elevator lines. In fact, it's not uncommon for the stairs entrance to have no line at all. The stairs terminate at the second platform, where you'll merge onto the elevator for the last leg to the top – at no extra cost, stairs tickets get you all the way to the top for less than half what an elevator ticket costs.

Not only are the stairs cheaper and skips the longer elevator line but the stairs route gives you an intimate look at the Eiffel Tower's rivet-and-steel guts, not to mention an inside-out view of Paris that you'll never forget. Go to "PILIER SUD" and look for the yellow sign advertising "ESCALIERS – STAIRS." From there, it's a mere 674 steps to the second platform. Onward ho!

24

The Eiffel's Lit!

I f all goes to plan, you'll catch the sunset from the top of the Eiffel Tower, then descend as darkness creeps in. At the bottom, hoof it across the Seine to the Jardins Trocadero for a spectacular view of what is perhaps the world's greatest night light. You see, after sunset, the Eiffel Tower turns on 20,000 sparkly lights that twinkle away every hour on the hour for five minutes. It's a beautiful, "Holy moly, I'm in Paris!" moment.

Installed in 1999 for the millennial celebration and still going strong (after having been replaced twice), hanging and powering all those twinkling lights required a Herculean effort. Just check out these stats:

- **25:** Number of mountain climbers employed during installation.
- **5:** Months it took those 25 climbers to hang the lights.
- **40:** Length in kilometers of strings of light and electrical cords.
- **10,000:** The total area in square meters of safety netting.
- **4.55 million:** The project's total cost in euros.

There are myriad ways to appreciate the Eiffel Tower, but the "*tour Eiffel*" is but the tip of the Paris iceberg. Let's dive deeper.

25

Orsay Evenings

T he Musée d'Orsay, or simply the Orsay, is Paris' pleasantest big art-museum experience. The Louvre is a heavy hitter and a mecca for art enthusiasts, but is an overwhelming, stuffy labyrinth of classical works that begin to all look the same after a couple hours. The Orangerie has Monet's famous water lilies and an idyllic location within Tuileries, but doesn't have an incredible breadth of works and is housed in a relatively ho-hum (for Paris!) building.

The Orsay, on the other hand, boasts an impressive depth of Impressionistic art – Van Gogh, Gauguin, Manet, etc. – and the building itself is a sight to behold. The only rub? Crowds. After the Louvre, the Orsay is Paris' most-visited art museum. Luckily, there's a workaround that, while it won't steer us completely clear of crowds, will get us through the Orsay with minimal pushing and shoving.

What's the trick? The Orsay stays open late every Thursday until 9:45PM. Keeping in mind your one-hour rule and the fact that the Orsay has tons to see, shoot for an arrival time of about 7:30PM, or just as the afternoon crowds and tour buses head to dinner. You'll waltz through a blissfully uncrowded Orsay until your belly reminds you it's time to make dinner plans. Or until security throws you out, whichever comes first.

26

Gargoyles on Your Shoulder

L egs still a little stiff from summiting those Eiffel Tower stairs? Rub on some Bengay and let's get ready for another ascent. After all, since you braved the Eiffel Tower's 674 stairs, you might as well surpass the thousand-stair mark by tacking on another 422 steps at Paris' Gothic heart-and-soul, the Cathédrale Notre-Dame de Paris.

While there are certainly higher and more famous viewpoints, nothing beats the view from atop Notre-Dame – the twisting lanes of the Latin Quarter fill the foreground while the Eiffel Tower stands sentinel in the background – it's the visual convergence of the medieval and gilded eras of Paris.

The view outward is just the beginning. Look around: Those gargoyles that seem so distant from ground level will practically be perched on your shoulders. It's an intimate look at Gothic construction. And some days, the bell tower is open for viewing – your chance to see "*l'original*" bell, the 13-ton "Emmanuel." Emmanuel is the largest of the cathedral's 10 bells and has been tolling since 1681. That's a hell of a long time. Chew on this: Emmanuel was already 200 years old when it rang triumphantly for Napoléon.

Luckily, there are now two ways to enjoy this view without waiting in line: reserve a spot in line using the JeFile mobile application or the reservation kiosks. Either way you choose (choose the app), reservations must be made day-of (no plans to expand the service for advanced bookings). So, while you're still subject to the early bird eating the worm and what-not, you can now at least pick a time and show up at that time, bypassing the line altogether. Rejoice!

Even though the tower doors don't open until 9:00AM, reserve a place in line as early as 7:30AM using the JeFile mobile application or promptly at 9:00AM (rest easy morning glory, cafés across the street sell emergency coffee and croissants) at the reservation kiosks located right outside the tower entrance on Rue du Cloître Notre-Dame – make an immediate right after exiting the cathedral.

Since day-of morning times will likely be booked via app users by the time the kiosks open, I recommend the app – download it for your Android or Apple phone at least the night before, then over breakfast open the app immediately at 7:30AM to reserve your desired entry time. Even after a long, leisurely breakfast, you'll still have an opportunity to tour Notre-Dame Cathedral before ascending the stairs at your reserved time slot.

Waiting in this line used to be a miserable hour-plus itinerary pothole, but the JeFile app smoothes over all that waiting and keeps your Paris day humming along. Now, to convince Parisian cafés to embrace this system for their outdoor tables...

27

Organic Notre-Dame

Y ou're not done with Notre-Dame yet, or, rather, Notre-Dame's not done with you. You've explored her wonderful nave and awesome roof and admired her gargoyle-bedecked facade; now, it's time to hear her sing. It won't cost us a dime.

Notre-Dame's organ boasts 8,000 pipes, some of which date to the 18th century. This is no ordinary organ; it's lived quite a life. The cathedral's first organ appears in historical documents as early as 1357. The present organ originates from 1730-33 and was renovated and extended in 1783-88. During the years 1959-68 the instrument was electrified, extended and reharmonized, losing its symphonic character and effectively ruining it. In 1990-92, a large-scale restoration was carried out, returning the organ to its symphonic character of the 19th century. In 2012-14, the organ was again restored with major modern updates, including installing a new computer traction, repairing the sunken pipes and cleaning the organ – all 8,000 dusty, dirty pipes.

The organ sounds off for the public every Sunday at about

4:30PM. Arrive a little early to find a seat. Get comfortable and zen out. You can't help but tingle listening to the organ music bounce around this Gothic church. It's a memory you'll never forget.

28

Ascending Montmartre

You exit the Anvers Metro station, thinking you've pretty much made it to Sacré Cœur, only to run smack dab into the stairway from hell that stands between you and the entrance to the bleached basilica. You've already climbed Notre-Dame and the Eiffel Tower on foot, so the dogs are a-barking and you've got to save stamina for Sacré Cœur's dome climb. It's one thing to climb a dome or a church tower, but surely there's a better route up Montmartre.

Don't fret. There sure is. Perhaps by now you've noticed a quaint funicular plying the Butte Montmartre roughly parallel to the stairway from hell. This little engine that could has been running since 1900 (it's been rebuilt twice since) and shuttles over two million passengers annually. In addition to providing a much-needed lift to would-be Montmartre pilgrims, there are two very cool things about this funicular.

Cool thing #1: It's a unique beast. Whereas most funiculars in the world rely on the opposing car for a counterbalance – which means one car must always being going up when the other is going down, and if one car breaks, then both are shut down –

the Montmartre funicular cars each have their own independent counterbalance. This is important because many more people use the funicular to go up than to go down (I prefer walking back down, too). So, when boarding lines become congested, the operators can switch both cars to uphill mode, doubling capacity and halving your wait time.

Cool thing #2: You can ride using a "T+" ticket from your previously purchased carnet. That's right – you can ride the funicular using the same tickets as you use on the Metro. The funicular is run by RATP, Paris' transportation authority, so your bus and Metro tickets are valid. Just zoom past all those suckers hoofing it over 300 steps up the hillside and bypass the funicular ticket-buying line. Flash a Metro "T+" ticket: Montmartre, here you come.

29

The Apex of Montmartre

T hanks to that calf-saving funicular, you're now at the top of Montmartre! Well, almost.

That feeling of standing outside Sacré Cœur's alabaster façade and turning to face the sea of Paris spread out below you probably fooled you into thinking your climbing was over. Not so fast... look up. Those iconic domes are to Sacré Cœur what the towers are to Notre-Dame. And like Notre-Dame's towers, you're going to take a closer look.

Sacré Cœur's 300-step dome climb is a total gas (what dome climb isn't?). While the route up Notre-Dame's towers is mostly indoors, Sacré Cœur's climb weaves inside and outside, up the basilica's archways, rooflines and hidden stairwells.

But to get up, first you have to get down – the dome climb's entrance and ticket window is downstairs and to the left of the main entrance; the line moves quickly. That ticket machine on the right is mostly for show, but in the rare event that it's actually working, use it instead of waiting at the ticket window (though both lines converge nearby at the climb's entrance).

30

Paris' Quirkiest Museum

The Museum of Hunting and Nature is not one of Paris' big-name museums, but that's a good thing and I guarantee it's well worth squeezing in the hour or so it takes to study this curious collection.

The Musée de la Chasse et de la Nature, located in an opulent classical mansion near the Pompidou Centre, contains a vast collection of hunting weapons and equipment, stuffed trophy animals and hunting ("*chasse*") and nature art. It stands as Paris' quirkiest museum, paying homage – amusingly at times – to big-game hunting's 19th century apogee. It also examines the negative impact of sport hunting on indigenous cultures and the environment. Well, expect at least a smattering of the latter.

It's a first-rate collection of the peculiar. From a costume-jewelry bedazzled stuffed Chihuahua to an animatronic albino boar head, this museum wastes little space, packing in the oddities and curios from a bygone era.

What's that? Yes, I said animatronic albino boar. Say hello to the albino boar head mounted in the Trophy Room and it may just say hello back! Just kidding, it doesn't vocalize, but it sure looks like it's trying to as the motorized eyes survey the room and the automated mouth opens and closes. What's it attempting to say? It's like Paris' version of the Big Mouth Billy Talking Bass, except mute. Did I mention this place is quirky? It's strange and totally engrossing. In other words, it's a total gas and the perfect antidote to art-museum fatigue.

31

The Louvre's "Super-Secret" Entrance

E ntering the Louvre increasingly feels like clawing through airport security. Bag checks, metal detectors, x-ray machines, armed sentries and crazy-long lines of selfie-pole clattering tourists congest the "glass pyramid" entrance, the Louvre's iconic main gateway. You should exit through the glass pyramid, but as for *entering* the Louvre, good news, there's a better way.

You'll skip the mandatory security line at the pyramid entrance and enter through the Carrousel du Louvre mall entrance at 99 rue de Rivoli – look for the red awning. You're still subject to the same security search as the main entrance, but... no one's here. The rue de Rivoli ingress is totally legit and spits you out at the same ticket lobby as the main entrance (directly under I.M. Pei's pyramid), but in only a fraction of the time.

Tourists (who don't own this book) flock to the glass pyramid, unable to resist its magnetic pull, while tour buses deposit their hordes directly in front of the pyramid entrance, so it's always swamped with humanity. The rue de Rivoli entrance, on the other hand, remains somewhat secret, so let's keep this between us. Deal?

Bonus tip: The shopping arcade below the Louvre has an excellent food court with delicious, affordable treats from around the world in a casual setting. I know what you're thinking: Eating at a food court while in Paris, are you crazy? Don't mock – this ain't your American food court. Hit the crêpe cart, dig into a whole-roasted chicken, sip gazpacho or try some tikka masala. Paris' version of a food court offers a delightful, quick bite before or after a lengthy Louvre mission.

32

Sunny Sainte-Chapelle

The Louvre's main rival in terms of long security lines has to be Sainte-Chapelle. The reason is simple: It shares a home with France's Supreme Court, the Palais de Justice. Unfortunately, no alternative entrances exist, so try Chapelle in the early morning or late evening when the light is best.

Yep, I'm advising you to time your visit with the light.

Instead of beating the crowds, you're going to follow the sunshine to see Chapelle's 14th-century Gothic stained glass, perhaps the world's best stained-glass windows remaining from the Medieval Era. 1,113 scenes from the Old and New Testaments recount the history of the Western world preceding Sainte-Chapelle's construction, which, amazingly, only took about seven years to complete. Contrast that with the roughly 180 years required to build Notre-Dame. Sufficiently impressed yet?

Chapelle's 15 towering stained-glass windows – 6,500 square feet of it – are best appreciated on a clear, sunny morning or evening when the light hits the windows just so. Look up and enjoy, basking in the Crayola-tinted sunshine.

33

See Napoléon First, as He'd Want It

You're going to oblige Napoleon's ego, for even in death the man casts his conceited shadow.

Hit a line, though rare it may be, at the Musée de l'Armée/Invalides? Simply go around the main entrance toward the golden-domed rear entrance adjacent to Napoleon's tomb (it's well-signed) for the museum's very-nearly secret entrance and ticket counter beside the museum café.

Most visitors enter the museum from the esplanade des Invalides – it's closer to the Invalides Metro station and where the tour buses generally deposit their charges. This rear entrance, however, is accessed from Place Vauban, takes a few minutes longer to reach from the Metro and doesn't attract the tour buses. And just like the main entrance, you can purchase tickets and access the full museum.

The amazing collection of French military history is the main draw here, but by entering through this secondary entrance you might as well oblige Napoléon's outsized ego and go see the little guy's tomb first, which is exactly how he'd want it.

34

Art Trains to Versailles

I n Paris, there's no escaping the art. Try as you might, the art is literally everywhere – from the Art Nouveau Metro signs to street artists. Nowadays, not even trains are safe from the art!

Art in Transit, an ongoing project since 2014, redecorates ordinary train-car interiors with recreations of Impressionist art and stained glass from the Musée d'Orsay. The latest installment features a second edition of Versailles-themed décor inside five cars on the RER C train line that connects Paris with Versailles. Art museum meets rolling stock for the 45-minute journey to Versailles.

Catch the 8:00AM RER C train to Versailles Château–Rive Gauche anywhere along the line in Paris – Invalides, Champs de Mars and Musée d'Orsay are popular stations. Only five of the 20 cars are decorated, so board well before departure, locate the decorated cars and secure yourself the prettiest view – the interior view, that is.

35

Don't Forget Your Passport

B efore you enter the Palace of Versailles (which I believe is French for "over-the-freaking-top opulence"), make sure you've got your passport. Your Versailles Passport that is!

Sorry couldn't help it. But seriously, for the full Versailles experience – including all three tours, musical fountain and garden shows and access to all special exhibitions – it pays to buy the Versailles Passport. In fact, you'll save about 50% over buying individual tickets.

The Passport comes in single-day and two-day increments. If you're a meticulous sightseer open to spending more than one day in Versailles, then the two-day Passport only costs a few euros more. There's a lot to see here, so consider it. Either Passport can be purchased at the ticket office or online. I highly, highly recommend purchasing online since the Versailles ticket lines can become interminable.

Versailles is a collection of attractions, the star attraction – the palace – is a single component within the full Versailles experience. You'll also want to check out the Trianon Estate, the gardens and the legendary musical fountain shows. All are covered by the Versailles Passport. Buying those tickets ad-hoc will cost about double what the Passport costs, so when in Versailles, bring your Passport.

36

A Wax Museum You Won't Immediately Regret

D o not waste time or money at any of Europe's wax museums. You will inevitably wade through an inexplicably long line only to pass through a gift shop cleverly disguised as a wax-figure museum. "Oh, hey look, it's a wax Geraldo Rivera. What a mustache!"

Every single one of Europe's wax monstrosities are – without exception – overpriced tourist traps pandering to the lowest common tourist denominator. Phew, I'm glad I got that off my chest. I feel better now.

Okay, so there's one exception. And a mighty exception it is. Paris' Musée Grevin is the bomb.

Somewhere lost in the shuffle of Paris' high-brow art, history and cultural museums you find the historic Musée Grevin, the wax museum that started it all (so blame them!). With its crazy baroque architecture and trippy mirrors, it remains a cut above the rest. Lose your grip on reality in the Hall of Mirrors, created for the 1900 Universal Exhibition.

Don't get me wrong, Musée Grevin is still cheesy and overtly touristy, like other wax museums. After all, it's had to compete with the likes of Madame Tussauds for decades. But a visit to Grevin comes with a smattering of history, harkening back to a time when halls of mirrors blew the mind, and a cheeky curiosity.

I recommend only one wax museum in Europe – this is it. And don't worry, you won't run into a wax Geraldo Rivera – Europeans don't know who he is and the artificial inhabitants here are a cut classier than in those tourist-trap wax halls. Think movie stars, historical figures, world leaders and rock 'n' roll luminaries, not Fox News or reality television nincompoops. Except that one guy, probably. You know the one.

37

Sundays are for the Birds

Let's flock to where the tourists aren't! So, don't be a bird brain and migrate over to the Sunday Bird Market, conveniently perched beside Cité Metro station and nested just a few hundred meters as the crow flies from Notre-Dame Cathedral.

Normally a fragrant flower market, housed in two 1900s-era glass pavilions, the Marché aux Fleurs et aux Oiseaux has been in the flower ("*fleurs*") hawking business since 1808, but transforms every Sunday into a squawking bird ("*oiseaux*") market perfect for a post-Notre-Dame or post-Sainte-Chapelle gander.

Even if you're not in the market for a bird – *and what traveler in their right goddamn mind is in the market for a bird?* – Paris' Sunday Bird Market is a pheasant way to spend a Sunday morning. (Okay, I admit that last one was a stretch.)

</bird puns>

38

Hunting Ninja Turtles

aris is awash in tours – private tours, group tours, shopping tours, foodie tours, family tours, bike tours, bar tours, architecture tours. Hell, there's even helicopter tours for the seriously well-funded vacationer (... *take me with you!*).

Of all Paris' tour choices, however, the sewer tour – yes, *sewer* tour – is Paris' most-overlooked guided journey. You'll explore over 500 meters of working Parisian sewer system at Musée des égouts de Paris. It's strangely fascinating, and a nice afternoon escape from the summer heat. Don't worry, you'll be on walkways above the sewage, so no need to pack the rubber boots. But do wear closed-toe shoes.

The self-guided tour explains how the sewers were originally built, maintained and upgraded over the years, with retired machinery and realistic mannequins adding a creepy element of realism to the caverns. Signs along the way indicate your above-ground location.

So while I'll never turn down an unlikely offer of a helicopter tour, I'll always make time for the Parisian sewers. And that's something I'd never thought I'd say.

39

Free Look at a Writer's Life

W ho doesn't love adding a few free attractions to the itinerary? After all, a euro saved is a euro earned, which is a euro that can be spent on wine later tonight.

The tiny Victor Hugo museum at 6 Place des Vosges offers an intimate and totally free look at Hugo's writing space, his process and lifestyle. Unsurprisingly, it's especially interesting for writers and fans of Victor Hugo as well as 19th-century furniture enthusiasts. It's a fun, low-key (read: group tours don't go here) hour hidden in plain sight on Paris' otherwise bustling Place des Vosges.

And did I mention it's free? After buying an eye-poppingly expensive drink at one of the Place des Vosges' timeless cafés, you'll be ready for something, anything free to assuage the financial sting. "Well, the espresso was 15 euros but Hugo's house was easily worth 10!" Isn't the rationalizing human mind brilliant?

40

Best of Bastille Day

I f you find yourself in Paris on Bastille Day – France's national holiday, celebrated annually on July 14 – then go brave the crowds at the Champ de Mars for the most iconic viewing point of Paris' famous Bastille Day fireworks display.

The Champ de Mars, the Eiffel Tower's adjacent park, is the hands-down, absolute best place to view the elaborate fireworks show that marks the celebration's crescendo. The fireworks burst behind and above the iconic Eiffel Tower, framing an impossibly breathtaking display. Just beware: Spectators start staking their spots in the morning.

Sure, there are plenty of places to watch the fireworks, but witnessing the display envelop the Eiffel Tower is a once-in-a-lifetime experience you'll remember forever.

41

Statue of Liberty's Doppelgänger

I t's time for a scavenger hunt to find a replica of the Statue of Liberty. Okay, so there are actually three Statue of Liberty doppelgängers in Paris, one in both the Orsay and Arts et Métiers museums, but you're seeking the largest and most-secluded Lady Liberty.

If you're wondering why we'd be expecting to find the Statue of Liberty's alter ego in Paris, here's a quick refresher on America's most-iconic monument, the Statue of Liberty, aka Liberty Enlightening the World:

Designed by sculptor Frederic Auguste Bartholdi, France gifted the hollow, copper Lady Liberty to the US in recognition of the French-American alliance during the American Revolution.

She arrived in the USA in 350 pieces in June, 1885. The reassembly process was eventually completed on October 28, 1886. The 305-feet tall statue shows a woman who has escaped the chains of tyranny, symbolized by the broken chains at her feet. Liberty's right hand holds a torch that is a symbol of liberty and holds a tablet in her left hand that reads "July 4, 1776" (in Roman numerals), the United States' Independence Day. The seven rays of Liberty's crown symbolize the seven seas and seven continents of the world.

The reclusive replica resides on the unappreciated Île aux Cygnes, only a few minutes' walk from the Eiffel Tower. It's an almost-quarter-scale replica of New York City's Statue of Liberty, 22 meters tall and facing west in the direction of its NYC-based twin. Inaugurated on 4 July 1889, about three years after its US counterpart, it was given to the city of Paris by the Parisian community in America to mark the centennial of the French Revolution.

So there you go. You've come to Paris for the Eiffel Tower, yet your Instagram feed will now feature New York City's most-iconic monument. Such is travel!

42

It's All Downhill from Here

Père Lachaise Cemetery is a steep, winding, protruding-cobblestoned labyrinth of graves. It's practically a death trap. Hoofing it around here for a few hours is torture on the soles, Paris' version of the Bataan Death March... but (and you knew there was a but coming) as final resting place to famous writers, musicians and Parisians, it deserves its reputation as a must-see attraction. Besides, you can rest your feet WHEN YOU'RE DEAD.

Hold on, though. There's a smart way to visit Père Lachaise and there's a dumb way. The smart way is to walk the downhill route with a cemetery map. The dumb way? Um, it's to do it any other way.

Take the smart route and give yourself (and your feet) a massive break by arriving at the Gambetta Metro station, uphill from the famed graveyard. Even though it's a bit further from the cemetery than the eponymous Père Lachaise station, Gambetta drops you off at the top of the cemetery by the entrance on rue de Rondeaux, known as the Porte Gambetta. From there, the walking is all downhill.

Bonus tip: Make a quick stop at one of the myriad flower shops outside the cemetery for a grave-marker map. You're going to need it in this beautiful tangled maze of death. Top sights here include the graves of rocker Jim Morrison and writers Oscar Wilde and Gertrude Stein, all three of which are closer to the Porte Gambetta entrance than the Porte Principale gate down the hill – another good reason to start at Gambetta.

43

Paris on Sale

L ike so much of daily life in Paris, even sales are regulated by the government. That's right, the "gubmint" regulates when retail shops can hold big sales. I know, I know. Yes, the French economy is stuck in 1951. No, that won't change anytime soon.

If you time your trip right, then you can reap huge savings during Paris' twice-annual sales. These sales usually last 4-6 weeks and are not to be missed since even high-end designer labels will slash prices up to 80%. Winter sales start in January, sometime after Christmas, while the summer blowouts kick off in late June and last until the city escapes for the August sabbatical. Look for the ever-ubiquitous "*soldes*" signs and follow these tips to guarantee happy, productive bargain hunting:

- **Plan ahead:** It's said that locals begin trying on clothes and getting their lists ready before the sales even start. As tourists, you may not have that opportunity but you should scope out exactly what areas of Paris you want to shop (the Marais is a popular choice) and exactly which department and boutique stores you plan on perusing.

- **Go mid-week and go early:** Locals and savvy tourists avoid the first few days of the sales and prefer to shop during the week to avoid weekend crowds. Regardless of what day you venture out, be sure to start early. Most shops awaken around 10:00AM.

- **Wait for the second price reduction:** If your schedule allows, the second and third weeks of "*les soldes*" offer the best value. Popular sizes are still available and prices are down 20-40%.

- **Try before you buy:** Most sale items are not returnable. Be sure to try on all your clothes and carefully read the fine print.

44

Shopping for Picasso's Pastels

W hile most tourists, especially those with a literary bent, go crazy for a faithful reproduction of the famous Shakespeare & Co. bookstore (it's a FAKE!), there's a more authentic shopping experience if you're in the mood to rub shoulders with long-gone cultural titans. I'm mean, still stop by Shakespeare & Co, but first peruse a little slice of art heaven at Magasin Sennelier, in operation continuously since 1887.

Even if you're not an artist, chances are you know someone who would just die for art supplies from this world-renowned art supplier. The building itself is enough to swoon over with exposed timbers, immaculate display cases and a "just-so-Paris" façade that will draw you in. Oh, and once inside! An explosion of paint, brushes, canvases, oak easels and much more awaits. History, too.

That box of "Couleurs du Quai Voltaire" paints you're holding? They were refined by Paul Cézanne. And those oil pastels you're considering? Picasso himself guided their creation.

You may have entered Magasin Sennelier thinking you

couldn't possibly need anything from here. You're just looking! You're only here because this book told you it was cool! Tourist, thou doth protest too much. Once the romantic-artist atmosphere sufficiently permeates your subconscious, you'll leave with some pens, pencils, paintbrushes and notebooks in tow – the allure can't be resisted. After all, Degas shopped here. Chanel designer Karl Lagerfeld still does. You can, too.

III

PART 3: INDULGE

45

Restaurant 101: Tipping & the Bill

You're going to eat well in Paris – be it at high-end sit-down restaurants or to-go crêperies. The dining options are astounding but before diving into this culinary cornucopia, let's go over what to expect from a full-service Paris restaurant and a few basic rules of conduct.

First off, eating out in Paris is an experience – an experience quite a bit different from eating out in countries like the United States. In Paris, diners are expected to linger long over meals and drinks. If you make a reservation, then restaurants expect you to occupy the table all night – rarely do Parisian eateries expect a second seating during dinner service.

While it's usually acceptable to sit indefinitely at a café table, or in a restaurant, once you ask for the check you've announced that you are leaving. Leave you must. Conversely, waiters won't bring you the bill automatically like in most American restaurants – that's considered rushing the guest and extremely rude. You will have to ask for the check, so simply flag down your waiter and announce: "*L'addition s'il vous plait.*" AKA, "The bill please."

Note that there are two kinds of restaurants: "*Service compris*" (tip included) and "*service non-compris*" (tip not included)." In a city where waiters are paid a living wage exclusive of tips, you're much more likely to encounter "*service compris*" eateries, but it doesn't hurt to check the menu to confirm this.

Tipping seems to be a point of confusion for many Americans. It's perfectly okay to tip – few waiters in this world will turn down extra money. But it's not at all expected in "*serivce compris*" restaurants that, again, proliferate in Paris. Feel free to round up your bill to the nearest euro or add a few more euros on top of that if you feel service was exemplary... or you party was a particularly difficult table. You know who you are.

46

Eat Like a Local

I n Paris, eat like a Parisian. It's all part of the experience; otherwise, you could've just stayed at home and eaten at your neighborhood Applebee's. To do what the locals do and eat the way they eat, let's get used to light, coffee-and-croissant breakfasts, hearty café lunches and slow, exceptional restaurant dinners lasting late into the night. Doesn't sound so bad, right?

Here are a few more tips for eating like a Parisian (okay, or at least a seasoned Paris traveler):

At food stands, bakeries and delis, make clear whether you want your food to go or to stay. Order to go/takeaway: "*à emporter*" (AH ahm-por-tay). Order to stay: "*sur place*" (SUHR plass).

In a café, find your own table (unless a sign states otherwise) that isn't marked "*réservé*," and politely flag down a waiter when you're ready to order. Don't be miffed if you're not immediately approached by a waiter like in other countries – Parisian café waiters are trained to let customers settle in and await the customer's signal. For a meal, try to find a table already set with placemats and cutlery, or pick an empty tabletop if you're only having a drink. This isn't a hard-and-fast rule, but frenzied waiters will appreciate it.

While brasseries and cafés usually serve their lunch menu for dinner, sometimes with a handful of dinner-only options, proper restaurants go big. They serve a specific dinner menu and, if they do open for lunch, they will usually close for a couple hours between lunch and dinner service to flip the kitchen and prep for an amazing nighttime experience. And have a smoke break, of course.

Keep in mind a few key factors when choosing and eating at restaurants:

Firstly, I prefer restaurants with chalkboard menus written in French. The chalkboard means they're rotating specials around seasonal favorites and the freshest, best-possible ingredients. A menu written entirely in French (get your Google Translate app ready) says the eatery tailors to a primarily local clientele. That's two good signs.

Secondly, inquire about a dress code. Plan on wearing your finest duds when eating a proper Parisian dinner, but the restaurant may also require men to don a dinner jacket or such. Find out first, so you're not surprised.

Lastly...

47

Do You Have a Reservation? Part 2

S peaking of eating like a local, did you make a reservation? It's imperative to secure a reservation at every restaurant you're determined to try. Whether you swing by before the lunch crowd for an evening dinner reservation, call for a table the day before or book online a week in advance, you really should make dinner reservations in Paris. That goes double for high season – May to September.

Increasingly, albeit reluctantly, restaurants in Paris are joining the digital revolution and accepting online reservations. Start at a restaurant's website and Facebook page, but also search OpenTable and la fourchette (owned by TripAdvisor). Nowadays, a good number of highly regarded restaurants accept bookings through one or more of those aforementioned online options.

No reservation? Content to let the chips fall where they may? You daredevil. Here's my advice: Stroll the sidewalks, take your time and pop into different eateries to find that perfect menu and dining ambience... and maybe, just maybe, they'll have an available table.

48

Drink Wine Like a Local

U nless you're a bona fide oenophile or hunting for a specific varietal, order wine like a lot of Parisians: By simply ask for the house wine, "*vin de la maison.*" A restaurant's "*vin de la maison*" is usually the best bang for your buck, often costing less than mineral water. Restaurants find good, dependable wines for their house stock and buy a lot of it. A lot. That drastically reduces the price for consumers.

Is it good? Hell yes. In a blind taste test with a $100 bottle, you'd have an arduous time determining which is which. In fact, numerous studies show very little difference in $20 and $100 bottles of wine. More often than not, the maker of the more expensive wine spends the same on production as the cheaper wine, but much, much more on marketing. Hmm, can you taste the high-ROI marketing in that Bordeaux? For good wine at a good price, order like a Parisian and have the "*vin de la maison.*"

49

Tap Water, S'il Vous Plait

To accompany all that vino, soften the palette with tap water. Tap water – "*carafe d'eau*" – is free, unlike bottled or sparkling ("gas") water and perfectly safe to drink. Paris draws its tap water from aquifers deep beneath the ground. The water is mineral-rich and refreshingly clean. Unless you specify "*carafe d'eau*," the waiter will bring an overpriced glass bottle of mineral water by default. They're crafty like that.

50

Restaurant? Brasserie? Café?

While the lines seem to blur more every year, it's important to understand – "*en français*" – the differences between Paris' eatery types, so you have the right expectations before entering an establishment. After all, you don't want to be the TOTAL LOSER who tries to order a cassoulet at a pâtisserie. *Quelle horreur!*

Here's the traditional breakdown of Parisian eateries and what you can expect at each:

Restaurant: Slow service typified by the "meal experience". Table seating. Usually specialize in regional dishes. Most offer a fixed-price, multicourse "*menu à prix fixe*" or "*menu du jour*". Business casual attire, with jackets possibly required and reservations strongly recommended. Open late morning/early afternoon to late, often closed between lunch (11am to 2 or 3pm) and dinner service (6pm to 11pm-1am).

Café: Hot coffee, cold beer, bottomless wine. Prompt service. Table and bar seating, usually inside and outside. Primarily drinks, sandwiches, salads, quiche, other light meals. Open morning to late.

Brasserie: Prompt service. Usually offer atmospheric terrace seating. Open morning/noon to late. Literally means brewery, so think American "gastro pubs". Good for drinks, snacks and full meals. Simple menus with popular French plates – omelets, quiche, chicken, salads.

Bistro: More casual than a restaurant, but better food than a brasserie. Usually specialize in regional dishes.

Boulangerie: Bakery serving bread, desserts, quiche, sandwiches, sometimes salads and cured meats. No/minimal seating. Ideal for picnic supplies and on-the-go breakfasts and baguettes. Open early morning to late afternoon/early evening.

Pâtisserie: Bakery specializing in pastries and sweets. Open morning to late evening/early night.

Crêperie: Specializing in crêpes, pancake-like French staples eaten for lunch and dinner, and galettes, the filling buckwheat version. Usually minimal seating. Open lunch to dinner.

Fromagerie: Cheese! Delicious "*fromage*" from around France – sweet goat cheeses ("*chèvre*") to tangy Roquefort. You're welcome to request samples before buying. Open morning to evening.

Charcuterie/Traiteur: Delis serving hot food, cured meats, quiche, salads to-go. No seating. Great for picnic supplies. Usually have drinks, wine. Open morning to evening.

Boucherie: Butcher's shop. Usually uncooked cuts but sometimes also cured meats like salami. Open morning to evening.

Cafétéria: Self-service cheap eats, food-court or buffet style. See the food before you order it. Perfect for hungry teenagers, impatient little ones and tightwads. Open early to late, depending.

Marché: Market, typically outdoors with temporary stalls serving fresh and prepared foods. Open morning to afternoon.

Supermarché: Supermarket. Indoor, one-stop shop like in America. Good for paper products, silverware, cups, wet wipes, cold drinks, etc. Usually open early to late.

L'épicerie: Mini-mart, small grocery, general store. Selection can vary widely. Usually open early to late.

L'épicerie Fine: Gourmet food shops, high-end mini-delis with hot and cold foods. Great for picnic supplies, or complementary items like salads, crackers, olives, caviar, chocolate mousse. Usually open morning to evening.

51

Subsidized Baguettes

Want to hear something that drives most Americans (and, to be fair, many Europeans, too) completely bonkers? The government regulates the price and ingredients of plain, traditional baguettes. No, I'm not kidding.

These delicious staples of everyday French consumption shouldn't cost you more than 1.10ish euros, making it BY FAR the best bakery deal. Bakeries ("*la boulangerie*") can charge whatever they please for fancier baguettes, and they do, but no one can price their traditional baguette above the government-set maximum. After waiting in an inevitable line, confidently tell the clerk: "*Une baguette tradition, s'il vous plaît.*"

Bonus tip: At a boulangerie, always order one type of item at a time, i.e. baguettes first, then croissants, etc., so the clerk can find your item and place it by the register.

A traditional baguette, a wedge of stinky cheese and a bottle of wine comprise the simplest and cheapest Parisian picnic. You can thank the government for that.

52

(Almost) Secret Picnic Spots

There's one and only one problem with picnicking in Paris: Everyone's doing it, man. Everyone wants to picnic on the Champs du Mars or Place des Vosges, but that's exactly the problem. There's always a crowd.

Well, it's not always a problem and I'm going to share with you my favorite places, where you can beat the crowds and picnic with plenty of space. Paris is replete with fine parks and public squares perfect for picnicking, but if you're in the mood for something a little less busy and more local, spread your feast at one of these lesser-known, but still easy-to-find and centrally located picnic spots:

Square du Vert-Galant on Île de la Cité is popular with locals, but remains mostly hidden from view under Pont Neuf. This miraculous little dose of serenity in one of the city's most bustling quarters makes a most memorable picnic location. Eat in the park itself or along the adjacent cobblestoned Seine promenade.

Rodin Sculpture Garden contains a little alcove in the back past the café. It has several oak lounge chairs, a sandbox for kids and, under the shade of the trees, is an ideal location to discreetly spread out a picnic.

The River steps outside the Orsay are a blast right after the museum closes. Pull out your bottles of wine, wedges of cheese, baguettes, salads, olives as you watch the sunset bounce off the Seine and the many gleaming buildings along its promenade.

Esplanade des Invalides right outside the Army Museum couldn't be more hidden in plain sight. Popular with area office workers for lunch and the occasional school group, it's wonderfully devoid of tourists, and always has a big patch of grass you can call your own.

53

Bière Here!

Some countries have regions called wine country, like Napa Valley in California. France – all of it – is wine country. There's no denying it. You're going to drink a lot of delicious wines while in Paris, but let's not forget about vino's hoppy friend, beer, a fermented beverage only now being adopted by Parisian brewers.

You see, Paris is no longer *just* about the vino. In fact, Paris hosts Beer Week every May if you happen to be in the vicinity. While France remains far behind its beer-swilling neighbors to the east, Paris is fast embracing a burgeoning craft-beer scene ("*bière artisanale*"). And no brewery celebrates this newfound passion for hops better than Brasserie La Parisienne. Take a behind-the-scenes tour (reserve ahead) or choose from a wide variety of pilsners, lagers and seasonals.

Finding good beer in Paris is no longer the struggle it used to be. Nowadays, it's as simple as saying, "*une bière s'il vous plaît*."

Please Leave a Review

Did you enjoy this book? Feel it was a strong value? Are you interested in leaving feedback so that I may improve future editions? If so, please leave this book a review on Amazon.

Leaving a review lets Amazon know that people are engaged and interested in this book and will help generate more exposure. There are millions of books on Kindle, so your review means a lot to help lift this title above the fray.

Thank you!

FREE Paris eBook

Receive a FREE Paris ebook today.

After downloading your free book, you'll receive a monthly VIP email with book giveaways, new book announcements and huge book discounts ONLY available exclusively to subscribers.

Join the crew and subscribe for FREE to Rory Moulton's monthly email newsletter about European travel, "EuroExperto." In addition to the giveaways and discounts, receive the month's best European travel articles, news, tips, trends and more. I'll never spam you. I don't do ads. And you can unsubscribe at any time.

Smarter European travel is just a click away: www.rorymoulton.com

About the Author

I'm a writer, editor, book author and entrepreneur living in the Colorado Rockies with my wife and son. When away from my desk, I'm passionate about travel, woodworking, museums and the great outdoors.

I believe and adamantly advocate that travel is most rewarding when done independently on a ground-level budget. Focus on experiential – not checklist – travel. Eat like a local. Stay in family run hotels, hostels or Airbnbs. Meet a local family. Picnic in the parks. Ride overnight trains. Sit in the cheap seats. Eat the street food. See the major cultural sights and prepare enough to avoid the tourist traps and lines, but also be spontaneous.

In short: Ditch the all-inclusive, find an affordable flight to a foreign country, fill a carry-on backpack and off you go!

Here are a few ways we can stay connected:

· Subscribe to my free, monthly email newsletter: rorymoulton.com/subscribe.
· Check out my books on Amazon, iBooks, Kobo and Nook.
· Catch up with me on Instagram @rorymoulton.
· Send me an email at feedback@rorymoulton.com.

I'd love to hear about your travels.

CPSIA information can be obtained
at www.ICGtesting.com
Printed in the USA
LVHW031917220419
615089LV00001B/91

9 780986 237874